LIGHT TRIUMPHANT

Esther Lense

LIGHT TRIUMPHANT

Copyright © 1977 by
The C.S.S. Publishing Company, Inc.
Lima, Ohio
Second Printing 1985

1253/ISBN 0-89536-301-1   PRINTED IN U.S.A.

LIGHT TRIUMPHANT

An Easter Vigil

Esther Lense

"Light Triumphant" is designed to go with the Good Friday Tenebrae service, "Out of Darkness Came the Dawn."

If you have not used the tenebrae, you will need to prepare the church for using this service. You will need seven individual candles and all the adornments usually on the altar placed on a table at the side and covered with a black cloth. You will also need to drape cross, altar, lectern, pulpit, and baptismal font in black.

The light in the church is still dim, as it was at the conclusion of the tenebrae service. None of the candles is lighted, although as many candles as possible are placed in the chancel area, to be lighted at the conclusion of the service. Also, as each person enters for the service, he is handed a small candle, to be lighted at the end. The various items which have been removed from the chancel are still on the table provided, and again members of the congregation will be utilized in restoring the church to its normal appearance. The flowers to be used in the Easter service should be readily accessible.

PROCESSIONAL HYMN: Come to Calvary's Holy Mountain

LIGHTING OF THE PASCHAL CANDLE
[The Paschal Candle should be ready, placed on the chancel, but unlighted. As the service begins, an assistant to the pastor shall come forward with a small lighted candle].

4

PASTOR: The Lord be with you.

RESPONSE: And with your spirit
PASTOR: We light tonight the Paschal Candle, symbol of the eternal light that shines forth through the merit of Jesus Christ, the Light of the World, the same Jesus Christ who was in the beginning and is today [**traces the sign of the cross**], he was in himself the beginning [**traces the Alpha**] and the ending [**traces the Omega**]. His are time [**traces the first numeral at the upper left angle of the cross**], and eternity [**traces the second numeral at upper right**]; his are glory [**traces the third numeral at lower left**] and dominion forever [**traces the fourth numeral at lower right**] and ever. Amen.

[**The pastor takes the small lighted candle from the assistant and lights the Paschal Candle.**]

PASTOR: May all the darkness of our hearts and minds be dispelled by the Light of Christ who rises on Easter morning in glory.
   The Lord be with you.
RESPONSE: And with your spirit.

The congregation is seated.

THE FIRST LIGHT: First Peter 3:18-19
   Why, Christ himself, innocent though he was, had died once for sins, died for the guilty, to lead us to God. In the body he was put to death, in the spirit he was raised to life, and, in the spirit, he went to preach to the spirits in prison.

   We have gathered together tonight to await the coming of the Easter dawn, and to celebrate in communion the most glorious day for Christendom, the day on which our Lord rose from the dead, so that we too may share in eternal life.

But this is still Saturday. What did Jesus do between the time that he was placed in the tomb on Friday evening and his appearance in the garden on Sunday morning? The words from the Epistle of Peter have told us.

The church teaches us that between his death and his resurrection, Christ descended to hell to preach to those souls who had never had the opportunity to learn of the New Way. In our Apostles' Creed, we repeat this tradition, as a part of our statement of faith. Who were these souls? This is one of the passages in the Bible which lays itself open to much interpretation. Perhaps they were the souls of those who had rebelled against God and perished in the Great Flood. Perhaps they were the fallen angels. We cannot say for certain. Nor can we give a time table for Christ's entry into hell.

But we may use as guides Peter's words in Acts 2:27, when he applied to Jesus the words of Psalms 16:10, "For you will not leave my soul among the dead, nor let your beloved know decay." And Jesus himself had applied to his ministry the great words of Isaiah 61:1, where the Lord's servant is sent "to proclaim liberty to the captives."

No doubt the early church was concerned with the questions of where Jesus was between the burial and the resurrection, and what was to happen to those who had died before the proclamation of the gospel. Christ, therefore, says Peter, brought this salvation into hell for the sake of those who had died without hearing the gospel and having the chance to repent.

Since Jesus, then, was alive in the spirit, although not yet in the body, we look to the beginning of the fulfillment of the promise, and remove the crepe from the cross.

6

[The pastor removes the crepe from the Cross. The first candle is lighted from the Paschal Candle. Throughout the service, all candles are lighted from the Paschal Candle. The lights in the sanctuary are gradually brightened, as before they had been gradually dimmed].

CONGREGATIONAL HYMN:
Alas, And Did My Savior Bleed

THE SECOND LIGHT: 1 Corinthians 5:7b
For Christ, our Paschal Lamb, has been sacrificed

Our altar lies bare and empty before us, ready for the sacrificial animal. But — no longer is it necessary for us to buy the perfect lamb, the pair of pure-white doves, to lay before the priest for him to offer as sacrifice in our name. Our Christ has offered himself as the sacrifice for all time. And so our altar need no longer be dripping with the blood of slain animals, no longer must the incense and smoke rise to Heaven. The sacrifice is complete.

And so, we return to the altar the paraments and the linen, making our altar pleasing to God in its beauty, and an everlasting symbol of the completed sacrifice.

[The paraments and linen are returned to the altar. The second candle is relighted].

CONGREGATIONAL HYMN: **I Lay My Sins On Jesus**

THE THIRD LIGHT: John 1:1-5
In the beginning was the Word; the Word was with God and the Word was God. He was with God in the beginning. Through him all things came to be, not one thing had its being but through him. All that came to be had life in him and that life was the light of men,

a light that shines in the dark, a light that darkness could not overpower.

What is the Word? The Word is the truth of the love of God for his creation, the Word is the light that brightens our weary way and gives peace and courage in darkness, the Word is the Son of God made man.

Without the Word, we are lost, stumbling our way through a hostile world. With the Word, we have guidance and a trustworthy help in all things. We therefore restore to the altar the Word of God, so that the proclamation of the Risen Lord may be made to all men.

[The Bible and missile stand are returned to the altar. The third candle is relighted.]

CONGREGATIONAL HYMN:
Bless Thou The Bread of Life

THE FOURTH LIGHT: Romans 3:23-25
Since all have sinned and fallen short of the glory of God, they are justified by his grace as a gift, through the redemption which is in Christ Jesus.

When the thief next to Jesus was hanging on the cross, Jesus offered him immediate entry into Paradise. Why? Not because he had done anything great; not because he had given a big donation; not because he was worthy in any way at all by earthly standards. But why? Because he had faith in Christ Jesus as the Son of God. And through his faith, he achieved eternal life. Jesus gave this promise freely, without pay, without any merit on the part of the thief. And again we may say, "Why?" And the answer is both beautifully simple and tremendously complex. Jesus could give the thief on the cross the immediate

8

entry into Paradise because he, himself, through his sacrifice, had paid any fees that might ever be expected.

There are no strings attached; there is no bargaining due on our part. Just faith. That's all our God asks of us.

But simply saying, "I believe" isn't enough. The Epistle of James tells us that faith without works is useless. And there are many ways in which we can show our faith through works. There are the many, individual, personal things that we can do for others. And there are the things that can be done in the name of the Church through our contributions of money and talents and time.

Therefore, we return to the altar the collection plates, not merely as representative of the collection of money, but also our contributions of all that we are, in whatever capacity we may serve. Our Savior gave even his life for us; we can in return give of ourselves to serve him.

[**The offering plates are returned to the altar. The fourth candle is relighted**].

CONGREGATIONAL HYMN: Just As I Am [vv 1-3]

THE FIFTH WORD: Matthew 22:34-40
But when the Pharisees heard that he had silenced the Sadducees they got together and, to disconcert him, one of them put a question, "Master, which is the greatest commandment of the Law?" Jesus said, "You must love the Lord your God with all your heart, with all your soul, and with all your mind. This is the greatest and the first commandment. The second resembles it: You must love your neighbor as yourself. On these two commandments hang the whole Law, and the Prophets also."

Many times we hear the words, "Jesus fulfilled the Law and therefore the Law is no longer binding for us." That's not true. Jesus fulfilled the requirements of the sacrificial aspects of the Law, and so we no longer need to sacrifice animals and birds in our churches. But the basis of the Law, whether Old or New Covenant, is **love**. Love for God, love for others, love for all of God's creation. And that basic law of love is binding on us. And how are we to know of this love unless we have the message of God and the proofs of his divine love proclaimed to us?

As we then rededicate ourselves to the proclamation of the Love of God made man, crucified for us, and resurrected for our sakes, let us uncover the pulpit and the lectern, the repositories of the mighty Word of God.

[**The pulpit and lectern are uncovered. The fifth candle is relighted**].

CONGREGATIONAL HYMN:
                    O Love That Wilt Not Let Me Go

THE SIXTH LIGHT: Romans 6:3-4
You have been taught that when we were baptized in Christ Jesus we were baptized in his death; in other words, when we were baptized we went into the tomb with him and joined him in death, so that as Christ was raised from the dead by the Father's glory, we too might live a new life.

As we come closer to the new day of Christian hope, the dawning of another Easter morning, we rejoice in the knowledge that because Jesus rose from the dead, we too shall in due time also rise into glory. This we know and this we affirm in faith.

But we are human, and sometimes we want visible symbols of the mysteries of faith. And so it is with our baptism. In baptism, our sins are washed away and we become truly God's children, through the gift of the Holy Spirit. This water which washes us is merely water such as we use every day for many purposes, but when it is used for this sublime washing away of our sins, it becomes the means of grace through which we receive forgiveness of sins, deliverance from death and the powers of evil, and eternal salvation.

As we uncover the baptismal font, let us reaffirm our baptismal vows.

[**As the congregation stands to renew the vows, the cover is removed from the baptismal font**].

PASTOR: Beloved in the Lord, on this most holy night the church, recalling the death and burial of the Lord Jesus Christ, is keeping vigil in love and, in the celebration of his glorious Resurrection, rejoices with great joy.

The Apostle Paul says:

> We are buried with him by baptism into death, that like as Christ was raised up from the dead by the glory of the Father, even so we also should walk in newness of life. For if we have been planted together in the likeness of his death, we shall be also in the likeness of his Resurrection; knowing this, that our old man is crucified with him, that the body of sin might be destroyed, that henceforth we should not serve sin . . . Likewise, reckon ye also yourselves to be dead indeed unto sin, but alive unto God through Jesus Christ our Lord.

[**The congregation shall stand throughout the reaffirmation**].

PASTOR: Let us then renew the promises once made in Holy Baptism, in which we once renounced the devil and all his works and all his ways, set forth our faith in God the Father, in Christ Jesus his Son, and in the Holy Spirit, and promised faithful service to God in his holy Church.

I therefore ask you:

Do you renounce the devil and all his works and all his ways?

RESPONSE: I renounce them.

PASTOR: Do you believe in God the Father Almighty, Maker of Heaven and earth?

RESPONSE: I believe.

PASTOR: Do you believe in Jesus Christ his only Son, our Lord, who was conceived by the Holy Ghost, born of the Virgin Mary, suffered under Pontius Pilate, was crucified, dead and buried; who descended into hell and the third day rose again from the dead; who ascended into heaven, and sitteth on the right hand of God the Father Almighty, from whence he shall come to judge the quick and the dead?

RESPONSE: I believe.

PASTOR: Do you believe in the Holy Ghost; the holy Christian Church, the communion of saints; the forgiveness of sins; the resurrection of the body, and the life everlasting?

RESPONSE: I believe.

PASTOR: Do you promise to abide in this faith and in the covenant of your baptism, and as a member of the Church to be diligent in the use of the means of grace and in prayer?

RESPONSE: I do, with the help of God.

PASTOR: May the almighty and everlasting God, who has vouchsafed to regenerate us by water and the

Spirit, and has forgiven us all our sins, strengthen and preserve us by his grace unto eternal life in Jesus Christ our Lord. Amen.

[**As the vows are completed, and the congregation sits, the sixth candle is relighted**].

CONGREGATIONAL HYMN:
Savior, Teach Me Day By Day

THE SEVENTH LIGHT: Matthew 26:26-28
Now as they were eating, Jesus took some bread, and when he had said the blessing he broke it and gave it to the disciples. "Take it and eat," he said. "This is my body." Then he took a cup and when he had returned thanks he gave it to them. "Drink all of you from this," he said, "for this is my blood, the blood of the covenant, which is to be poured out for many for the forgiveness of sins."

The time is almost here. Easter morning is rapidly drawing near. Easter morning, on which the tremendous achievement of Christ — the victory over death — is to be celebrated once more. As we come near to this moment, let us join together in the fellowship of the Lord's Table, repeating the sacrament which he gave us. We return the Communion service to the altar and join together in worshiping our Savior by remembering his sacrificial love for us. And as a symbol of the light which is about to return to the world, we light the seventh candle.

[**Whatever Communion service you wish may be used here.**]

CONGREGATIONAL HYMN: Just As I Am [vv 4-6]

THE COMMUNION SERVICE
[This should be timed so that the conclusion of the service of the Lord's Supper will come at midnight.]

THE LIGHT OF THE WORLD: John 8:12
When Jesus spoke to the people again, he said, "I am the light of the world; anyone who follows me will not be walking in darkness; he will have the light of life."

Easter morning has come once again! Once again we celebrate the Risen Lord! Alleluia! Alleluia! Christ is risen! He is risen indeed! Once more the shadows of the world have been driven away by the Light of the World. Once more we may rest secure in the knowledge that death has been conquered, that sin can be vanquished by the might of the Love of God made man.
Alleluia! Christ is risen! Christ is risen indeed!

CHOIR: Christ the Lord Is Risen Today
[As the choir sings, the altar candles are brought forward and replaced on the altar. They are then lighted from the Paschal Candle, and all the candles in the nave and chancel should be lighted. Acolytes [or youth] should then go down the aisles lighting the candles for each person at the end of each pew. There should be an acolyte for each end of the pew. The person whose candle is lighted then turns to the person next to him and lights his candle, until all the candles are lighted. As each candle is lighted, the person lighting it says, "Christ is risen." At the conclusion of the anthem, while all the congregation are still standing, with lighted candles, selected members of the congregation [including children] should bring foward the Easter flowers and place them on the chancel].

14

PASTOR: Once more we celebrate the dawning of yet another Easter. May the peace of the Risen Lord fill your hearts this day and through the days to come, that in your lives, your thoughts and your hearts, you glorify the Resurrected One, Jesus Christ, the same yesterday, today and forever.

And now depart in peace; the peace of the Lord go with you. Amen.

RECESSIONAL: **Alleluia! Jesus Lives!**

THE PASCHAL CANDLE

A

1   9

✚

7   ?

Ω

www.ingramcontent.com/pod-product-compliance
Lightning Source LLC
Chambersburg PA
CBHW071814020426
42331CB00009B/2497